CONTENTS

THE
RESISTANCE

By 1944 World War II (1939–1945) had claimed millions of lives and devastated much of Europe. But after five bloody years of war, the American and British-led Allied forces had gained the upper hand over the German-led Axis powers. Their success was due, in part, to the support received from Resistance fighters. These volunteers supported the Allied forces. They assisted in many ways. Resistance fighters sheltered pilots shot down in enemy territory. They offered medical assistance and helped the soldiers escape to safety. And, in many cases, the Resistance members worked as spies, gathering valuable information.

Unlike soldiers, most Resistance fighters were just normal people. Most didn't have special training, and they weren't always the best men and women for the job. But they did have a passion to protect their land and end the Nazi occupation of their countries.

GREAT ESCAPES OF WORLD WAR II

OUTRUNNING THE NAZIS

THE BRAVE ESCAPE OF RESISTANCE FIGHTER SVEN SOMME

by Matt Chandler

Raintree is an imprint of Capstone Global Library Limited, a company incorporated in England and Wales having its registered office at 264 Banbury Road, Oxford, OX2 7DY – Registered company number: 6695582

www.raintree.co.uk
myorders@raintree.co.uk

Editor: Anna Butzer
Art Director: Nathan Gassman
Designer: Ted Williams
Media Researcher: Wanda Winch
Production Specialist: Gene Bentdahl
Cover Illustrator: Pericles Junior
Illustrator: Daniele Nicotra
Colourist: Douglas A. Sirois

ISBN 978 1 4747 3214 7 (hardback)
21 20 19 18 17
10 9 8 7 6 5 4 3 2 1

ISBN 978 1 4747 3218 5 (paperback)
22 21 20 19 18
10 9 8 7 6 5 4 3 2 1

British Library Cataloguing in Publication Data
A full catalogue record for this book is available from the British Library.

Design Element: Shutterstock: aodaodaodaod, paper texture, esfera, map design, Natalya Kalyatina, barbed wire design

Printed and bound in India.

Sven Somme was one of thousands of members of the Resistance aiding in the defeat of the Nazis. He worked as a Resistance spy, secretly photographing Nazi war boats and troops behind enemy lines. Somme didn't come from a military background. He was a zoologist from a tiny town in Norway. Three of Somme's siblings were also in the Resistance, but it is the story of Sven Somme that is the most gripping. How does a man of no special skills or physical strength outwit the Nazis? How does he selflessly aid the Allies, escape a death sentence and travel 322 kilometres (200 miles), mostly on foot, to freedom?

RUN TO FREEDOM

Island of Otteroy, Norway, 1944

The work of the Resistance was incredibly dangerous. Anyone caught aiding the enemy was subjected to execution at the hands of the Nazis.

Sven Somme knew the risks better than anyone. His own brother, Iacob, was executed by firing squad in 1944 after being captured by the Germans.

I can't believe how many weapons they are stockpiling for the war.

Somme was very careful to go unnoticed as he photographed behind enemy lines. But on a particularly sunny day, sunlight reflecting off his camera lens caught the eye of the German soldiers on the docks.

Did you see that? There is someone hiding behind the cargo!

Impossible. Everyone is accounted for.

I know what I saw. We must investigate!

They've spotted me! I've got to get out of here, but there's nowhere to run.

With nowhere to escape, Somme hid his camera and walked away. He imagined he could blend in and pass for a stray countryman out for a stroll, instead of a master spy.

What are you doing out here? Where are you going?

I am a zoologist out for a walk. I did not know this place was off-limits. I will leave at once.

We could detain you for trespassing. We'll let you go, but consider yourself warned.

Moments later . . .

This belongs to him. I KNEW he was a spy. He is Resistance! Alert the men. He will not leave this island alive!

He left the camera, but he might still have film, maps or other contraband with him.

We cannot allow him to reach the Allied forces!

Somme returned to his safe house on the island. He alerted some other members of the Resistance that he was stopped and questioned.

My motorboat is my best chance of survival. If I can escape the island, I might make it to England.

Good luck, Sven. Be safe!

Somme ran the kilometres from the house to his motorboat on pure adrenaline. He could feel the soldiers closing in on him. It was a race for his life!

The boat! There it is! I can make it. Please let the old motor start.

8

9

Somme was to be held on board a German war ship under guard until the facts could be gathered. Then, when it was proven he was a spy for the Allied forces, he would be executed by firing squad.

You have an innocent man. I am a zoologist, not a spy. I was here to watch birds, not bombs!

I tell you, I am innocent. This is a mistake. Do I look like a spy to you?

If you were innocent you would not have hidden your camera. You are Resistance, and for that you will be executed.

You foolish dreamers of the Resistance. You'll soon find out what happens if you try to take on the mighty army. There will be no mercy.

10

It was decided the prisoner would be transported to a German military base. Somme knew what this meant — torture at the hands of the Gestapo. The stories of what the Gestapo did to prisoners were legendary.

This is crazy. Even if I escape, surely they will hunt me down and shoot me dead. Still, I must try for the Resistance!

Each time his guard left for coffee or to talk with a soldier, Somme focused on his escape. He began by spitting onto his cuffs and working to wiggle his hands loose.

As luck would have it, though, one of his guards had a moment of kindness and removed his cuffs.

This will help you sleep better. You can stretch out and relax.

Thank you. This is much more comfortable. You are kind.

This changes nothing. They are still going to execute you once we reach the base.

Somme knew the guard's words were true. He certainly would be executed because he was guilty of spying, and his captors knew it. They had the evidence.

The whole ship is filled with Norwegians. If I get past this guard, surely I can blend in with my fellow countrymen.

Somme took a deep breath, said a quick prayer and crept to the door.

It's unlocked?!

He stepped through the door and took the first steps towards freedom.

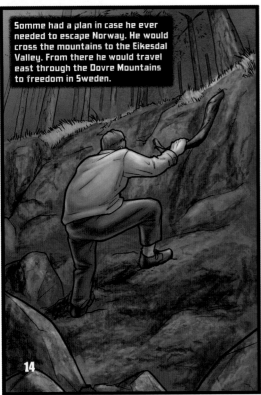

Somme had a plan in case he ever needed to escape Norway. He would cross the mountains to the Eikesdal Valley. From there he would travel east through the Dovre Mountains to freedom in Sweden.

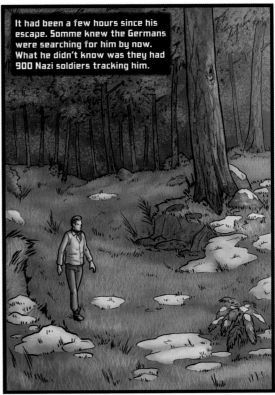

It had been a few hours since his escape. Somme knew the Germans were searching for him by now. What he didn't know was they had 900 Nazi soldiers tracking him.

15

It wasn't part of his original escape plan, but Sven Somme, the 40-year-old zoologist, was high up a tree, preparing to jump.

If I miss, I just hope the fall kills me, and it's over quickly.

Ahhhhhhhhhh!

Somme survived his first jump. Now he had to navigate the trees from above.

This would be a lot easier if I had decent shoes. Climbing trees in dress shoes is a recipe for death!

Fortunately, in many places, the trees were very close together. This allowed him to swing from tree to tree.

They've got to be closing in on me. Surely they can travel the ground faster than I can swing from trees.

After one last leap, the spy saw green grass below.

Unhhf!!

Ahhhh, silence. I've outrun the barking dogs and the Germans with their rifles. Still, they won't give up, I must keep moving!

The young woman was named Ragna. Her brother, Andre, and a friend wanted to help Somme. They had heard of his escape and knew hundreds of Nazis were hunting him.

We brought plenty of food and warm clothes for you.

The Germans have searched every home by now. Hopefully they won't come back around.

You cannot cross the mountains in those shoes. Try my boots to see if they fit.

Thank you. I truly don't know how to repay you.

Make it safely to Sweden and show those Nazis they can't mess with a Norwegian!

After several days of rest, Somme prepared to continue his journey. He began by writing a letter to a member of the Resistance.

Kristian, I want a new name, an identity card, a passport and some money.

He directed the Resistance to deliver the supplies to a safe house to the east. It was the next stop on his escape route.

Thank you again for your hospitality. I could not make it to Sweden were it not for you.

We'd better start hiking if we are going to make it to the precipice by dawn.

Just remember, Sven, when we encounter people, don't speak much. A quick hi is all. We don't want to raise suspicions. Everyone knows about the hunt for you.

As the three men hiked towards Somme's safe house, the mood was bright. The three Norwegians were sure that after a week the Germans had stopped searching for Somme.

I'll bet you can already feel freedom, Sven.

I didn't think I would make it this far. I was sure the Germans would capture me. Now, I'm sure they won't!

Ha ha ha!

Once they reached the snow-covered mountains, the group strapped on their skis.

This feels almost like a normal weekend! If only I had my gun, this could be just another hunting trip.

Except on this trip, you're the one being hunted.

Andre and his companion escorted Somme as far as the Finset Farm.

Good luck my friend.

Thank you both so much. Please, thank the others as well. I owe my life to you all.

The farmer, Nikolai, supplied Somme with clothes, food and other supplies.

We will get you across the canyon, but from there you will be on your own. It will be a 10-day hike to the safe house.

That is more than generous. Thank you.

It is our pleasure to aid a man loyal to the Allied forces.

Once he crossed the canyon, Somme bid his guides farewell.

Be safe and write to us from Sweden!

Indeed I will. Thank you!

He had escaped the search parties, but Somme wasn't out of danger yet. Norway was still occupied by the Germans, and he was a spy on the run.

I'm so close, but I'm one German away from being dead. I can't relax now, I've come too far to be captured!

After many more kilometres of hiking, Somme reached the Resistance safe house. Here he would rest and await the paperwork he needed to cross the border.

Sven, it is wonderful to see you. We didn't know if you would make it.

It was a harrowing escape, but I am a fortunate man. I have had much help along the way.

You must be so hungry. Let's eat!

The farmhouse was owned by Inga's brother, Hjalmar, who would help Somme prepare to enter Sweden.

You must stay hidden while you are here. The neighbours will talk and word cannot get out that you are here, or we'll all be in danger.

I'll do as you say. I can stay inside, undercover.

It was decided that Somme would be safest in the woods, away from the farmhouse. He lived there for nearly a month.

It will be a while before you can leave. The roads are filled with German troops. You would never make it.

I've made it this far. I can be patient.

Good. Very good.

To pass the time at the farm, Somme began to write his story.

Throughout the journey it has been fear that has kept me alive. I won't let the Germans capture me.

The journal would eventually become the basis for his autobiography *Another Man's Shoes*.

After a few weeks with the Resistance, Somme received a surprise visitor, his brother Knud.

You're alive! We were worried sick.

I was worried for a while too. But I am well. And you, Knud, are looking well also.

After a long wait, a package arrived with everything Somme needed to cross to Sweden. He now had money, a passport, ration cards and new clothes.

Please tell those who made this happen, thank you. Their work has saved me.

Yes, sir. Good luck.

23

Along with his package came a letter from the Resistance. It detailed the German soldiers' efforts to capture him.

Nine hundred Germans on my trail?! It's even worse than I suspected.

I can't use this passport or ID card. They've got my picture. The same one I'm sure the German's showed everyone. I'll be arrested for certain.

What will you do? It's too late to secure new documents. Your time is now.

I'll have no choice. If I'm asked for identification, I will have to shoot. I've not come this far to die, Hjalmar.

Realizing for the first time he may be forced to kill a man, Somme began to practise.

I'm not a killer. I can't shoot a man. But if it is life or death I will survive.

24

The British are dropping supplies to the troops in the mountains. We are so close, Knud. So close to being home.

When will this war end? Hasn't enough blood been shed?

Word had come through the Resistance that it was time for Somme to move on. Inga prepared a feast for his last night.

You'll find the rowing boat at the river's edge. Row across the lake and you'll meet Jorgen. You're almost home, my friend.

You have been too generous. I won't forget this once I reach England.

As he had done so many times on the trip, Somme departed under the cover of darkness.

Thank you for rowing, Knud. I am quite exhausted from this journey. You are a good and loyal brother.

I'll be with you until my last breath, brother. We are Resistance!

This is it. I'm going to make it!

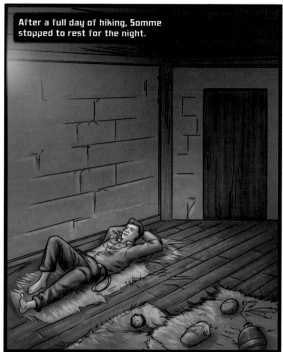

After a full day of hiking, Somme stopped to rest for the night.

For the remainder of his trip, Somme was assisted by a series of Resistance fighters. Each would feed and shelter him as he zigzagged his way across the Norwegian countryside to Sweden.

This meal is delicious. You are an amazing cook.

It is an honour to cook for you, Sven. Your work is so important. You are a hero to us all.

I've got maps and directions for you, but you must leave soon to keep on schedule.

You must meet up with John at the sawmill marked on the map. It is abandoned and you will be safe there for the next night.

Thank you, and your wife. You are brave and selfless heroes of the Resistance.

Somme's next guide offered him a bicycle to continue his journey.

After more than 160 kilometres on foot, this is incredible!

Finally, the end was near. Somme could almost see Sweden. But the final leg of his journey wasn't easy.

I've survived being hunted by 900 Germans, but these mosquitoes might be even worse! Surely I must be near the border.

As he prepared to cross over the border, Somme became nervous about the border guards.

I can't shoot a human being, even if they are going to kill me. I hope my conscience doesn't cost me my life.

But Somme had no need to worry. There were no guards. There were no Germans at all. There wasn't even a border crossing. After months on the run and hundreds of kilometres, Sven Somme calmly walked into Sweden. He was a free man.

HOME AND FREE

Sven Somme had no idea when he reached Sweden in 1944 that cancer would take his life before his 60th birthday. The man who had outwitted and outrun the Nazi's only had 17 years of freedom to enjoy. And enjoy it he did. After reaching Sweden, Somme was granted asylum, and he made it to London. There he was given a private meeting with the King of Norway, King Haakon, who was living in exile. Somme shared with the king his experience of escaping the Nazis. Settling in England, Somme married his British girlfriend, Primrose. Together they had three children, all daughters. Somme wrote a book detailing his life as a spy for the Resistance. *Another Man's Shoes* told the story of his capture and escape in great detail. It became his legacy following his death in 1961.

Decades later, one of Somme's daughters, Ellie, was cleaning out her mum's residence when she came upon a box. Inside she found letters, maps and other materials Somme had kept from his days as a spy for the Resistance. For Ellie, and the rest of Somme's family, it confirmed what they already knew. Sven Somme was a man who risked his life to free his country and protect Europe. He was a hero.

GLOSSARY

Allied forces countries united against Germany during World War II, including Great Britain, the United States, Canada, France and others

Axis powers group of countries that fought together in World War II; the Axis powers included Japan, Italy and Germany

contraband goods that are against the law to possess

detain hold prisoner

Gestapo secret police of Nazi Germany

Nazi member of the National Socialist Party led by Adolf Hitler, which controlled Germany before and during World War II

precipice cliff with an overhanging face

Resistance secret group of fighters that worked against the Nazis in occupied countries of Europe during World War II

safe house place where spies or other secret agents can go for help and protection

trespass enter someone's private property without permission

zoologist scientist who specializes in studying animals

COMPREHENSION QUESTIONS

1. What is the significance of the title for Somme's autobiography? Explain using details from the text to support your answer.

2. Considering his journey through the snow-covered forest, what would be another possibility for the title of Somme's autobiography? Use details from the text to support your answer.

3. Even though Somme was a Resistance fighter, the reader will notice that he doesn't seem to be perfectly suited for that job. How do we know this? Use details from the text to support your answer.

READ MORE

Another Man's Shoes, Sven Somme (Polperro Heritage Press, 2005)

Can You Keep a Secret?: Growing Up Under Occupation, Anne De Cintra (Uniform Press, 2016)

Stealing Nazi Secrets in World War II (You Choose: Spies), Elizabeth Raum (Raintree, 2015)

True Stories of the Second World War (Usborne True Stories), Paul Doswell (Usborne Publishing, 2012)

WEBSITES

www.bbc.co.uk/schools/primaryhistory/world_war2/world_at_war/
Learn all about the world at war at this BBC website.

www.ducksters.com/history/world_war_ii/
Check out this website to learn more about World War II, including spies and secret agents working during the war.

http://ww2db.com/battle_spec.php?battle_id=153
See photographs of members of the French Resistance, and learn more about the Movement at this website.

INDEX

TITLES IN THIS SET

BEHIND ENEMY LINES:
The Escape of Robert Grimes with the Comet Line

DEATH CAMP UPRISING:
The Escape from Sobibor Concentration Camp

OUTRUNNING THE NAZIS:
The Brave Escape of Resistance Fighter Sven Somme

TUNNELLING TO FREEDOM:
The Great Escape from Stalag Luft III